Disney · PIXAR
TOY STORY 2
Toys to the Rescue

A GOLDEN BOOK®
Golden Books Publishing Company, Inc.
New York, New York 10106
No part of this book may be reproduced or copied in any form without written
permission from the publisher. Produced in U.S.A.
Book printed in U.S.A.

We'd be happy to answer your questions and hear your comments. Please call us toll free at 1-888-READ-2-ME (1-888-732-3263).
Hours: 8 AM–8 PM EST. For US and Canada only.

ZURG

BUZZ

Rex blasts his way through a new video game.

Woody is going to Cowboy Camp with Andy. He tells the toys how to stay out of trouble while he's gone.

DRAW!

MEETING AGENDA

1. Moving buddy?

2. Plastic corrosion awareness meeting.

Mr. Spell

3. Andy's birthday party today.

4. Bubble wrap—don't pop.

"It's Cowboy Camp time!
We'll go hiking and horseback riding!"

Uh-oh! Woody needs some sewing.

He won't be going to Cowboy Camp after all.

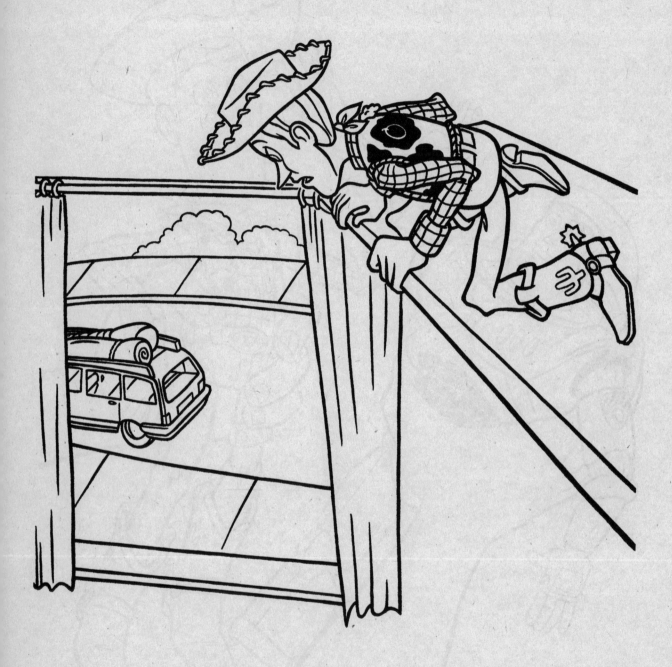

"Wheezy!
I thought Mom took you to get fixed months ago!"
Now mom is taking Wheezy to the yard sale.

Woody is off to rescue Wheezy!

Wheezy's been saved...
but now Woody is in trouble.

Woody's being toy-napped!

Buzz races after Al's car to try to save Woody.

Woody meets Bullseye and Jessie...

...and the Prospector.

Woody learns that he once was the star of the TV show *Woody's Roundup*.

The Prospector, Jessie, and Bullseye starred with Woody on the show.

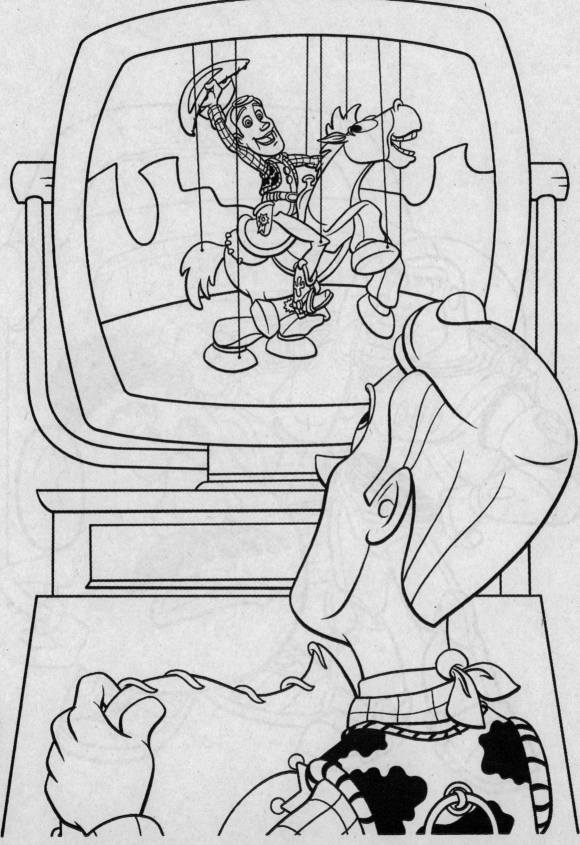

Meanwhile, Buzz tries to decode Al's license plate.

Woody finds out how famous he really was.

"Now we're a complete *Woody's Roundup* set!"

Oh no! Another accident with Woody's arm!

**Woody will have to try his escape
some other time.**

The Cleaner comes to help out.

Woody is as good as new.

"Kids grow up. And they don't want old toys," says Jessie.

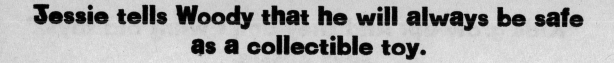

Jessie tells Woody that he will always be safe as a collectible toy.

Woody decides to stay with the Roundup Gang.

Buzz and the toys have found Al's Toy Barn!

But the busy street stands in their way.

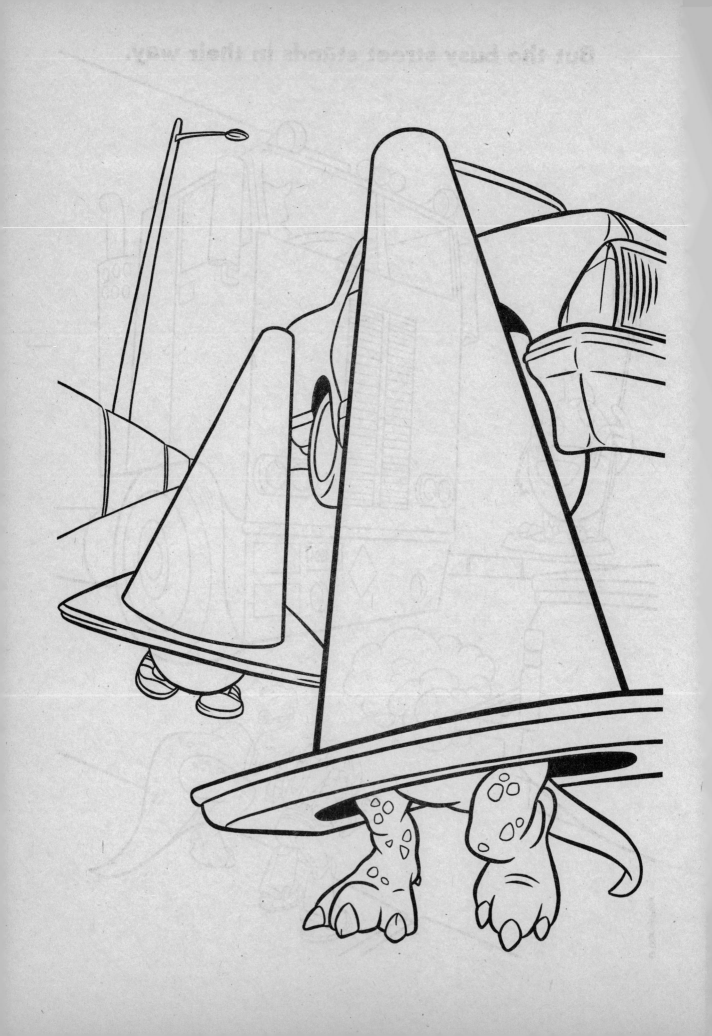

Buzz leads the toys safely across the street.

It's time to split up and look for Woody.

Rex finds the secret to defeating the evil Emperor Zurg.

Fasten your seat belts!

Fasten your seat belts!

Rex finds the secret to defeating the evil Emperor Zurg.

It's "New Buzz!"

"I could really use a new, improved toolbelt!"

"I place you under arrest for coming out of hypersleep without permission."

"Hey, you can't arrest me! You're just a toy. Let me out of here!"

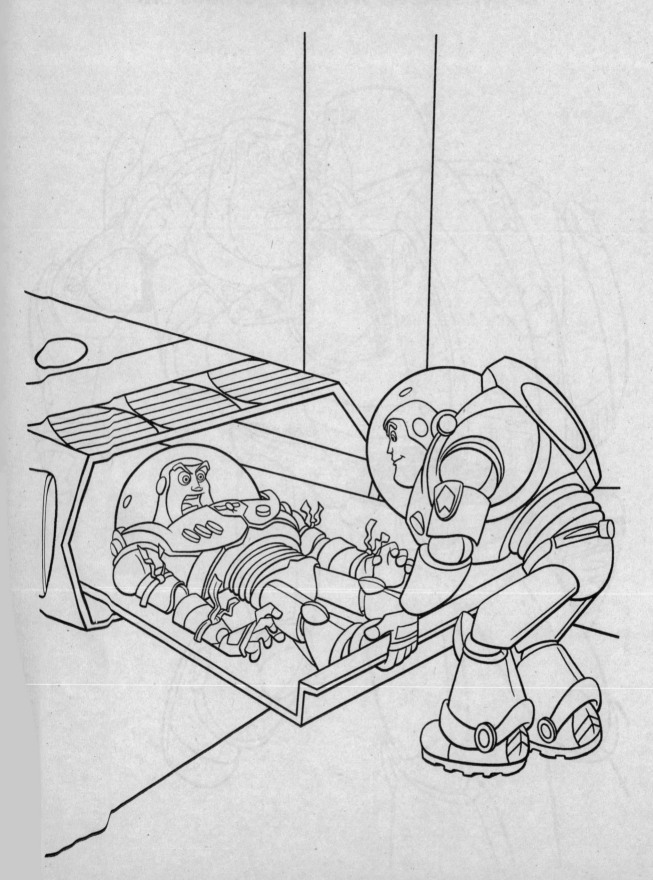

The toys don't realize they have the wrong Buzz.

The toys finally find Al's office.

But Woody's not there!

The toys hitch a ride in Al's bag.

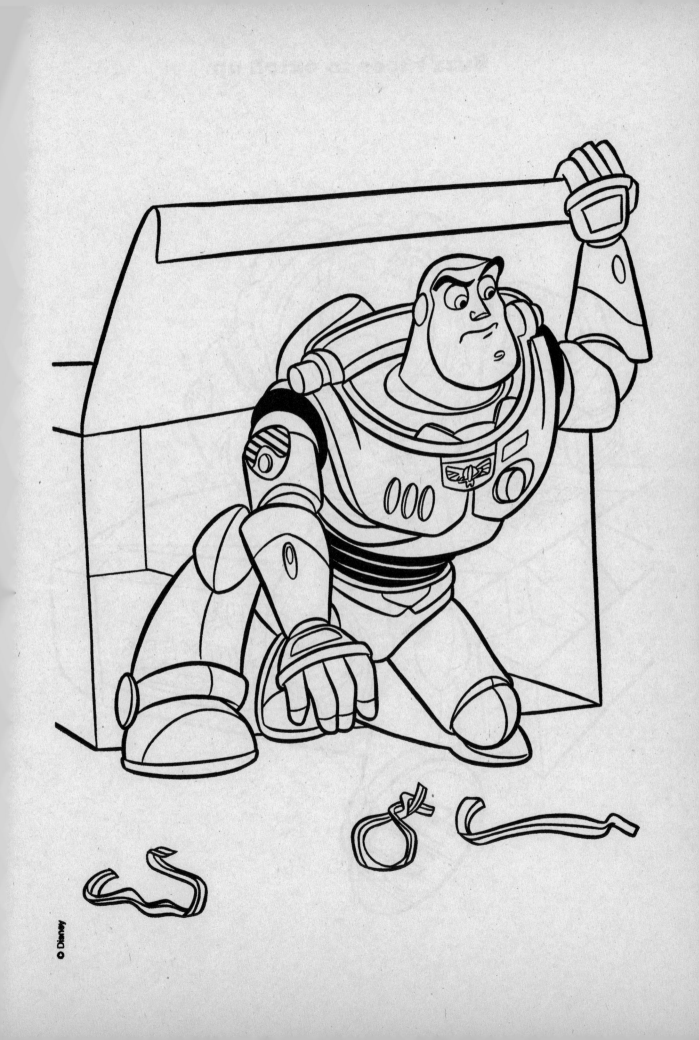

Buzz races to catch up.

Woody is having lots of fun with his new friends.

"We're here to bust you out, Woody!"

"Buzz! Guys! How did you find me?"

Andy's toys find out which Buzz is their real pal.

**"I'm staying," says Woody.
"Without me, they're stuck in their boxes."**

Connect the dots to add Prospector's hat.

The gang leaves without Woody.

© Disney

**Woody starts to miss Andy.
He wants to go home.**

Woody, Jessie, and Bullseye want to leave, but Prospector won't let them.

© Disney/Pixar

Al packs up the toys to go to the museum.

Al drives off! The toys must follow him to get Woody back. New Buzz decides to stay behind.

Al doesn't know he's being followed.

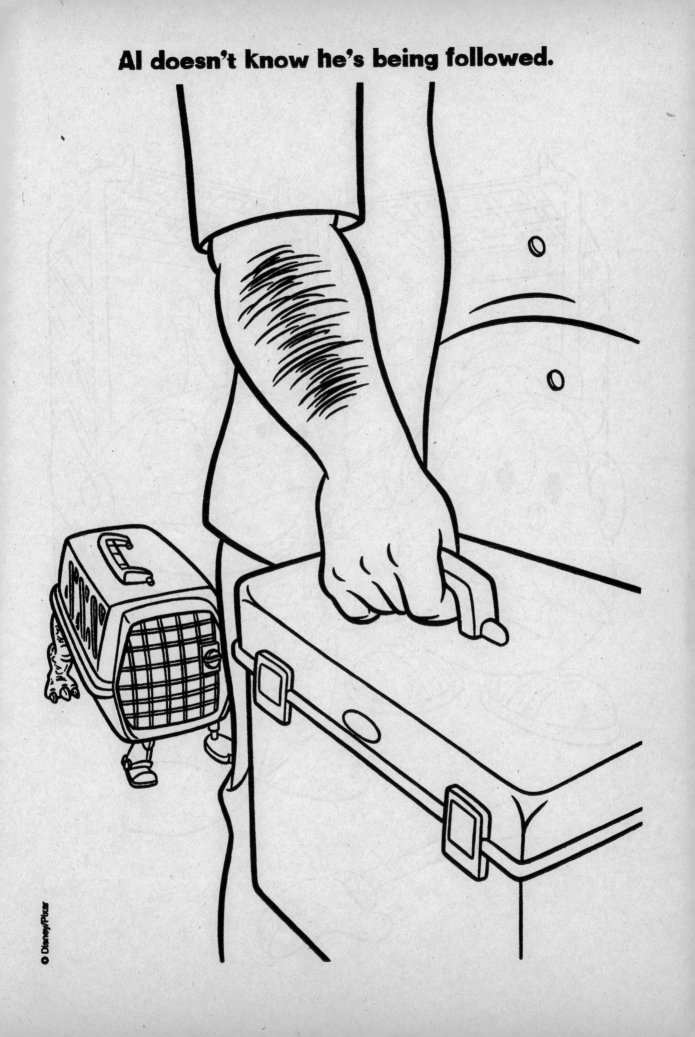

The toys try to find Woody.

The Prospector stands in the way of Woody's escape.

No more trouble from Prospector!

Who will save Jessie?

© Disney/Pixar

Buzz and Woody go into high gear.

It's Woody to the rescue!

There's only one way out of this plane.